Lessons From The Dojo

Applying Martial Art Wisdom to Overcome Fear, Anxiety, Anger, and Self-Doubt

Peter Tocco

www.petertoccoauthor.com

Samurai Publishing

Eastchester, New York

Peter Tocco/Samurai Publishing
Eastchester, New York 10709

Publisher's Note: Although the author and publisher have made every effort to ensure that the information in this book was correct at press time, the author and publisher do not assume and hereby disclaim any liability to any party for any loss, damage, or disruption caused by errors or omissions, whether such errors or omissions result from negligence or any other cause.

Adherence to all applicable laws and regulations, including international, federal, state and local governing professional licensing, business practices, advertising, and all other aspects of doing business in the US or any other jurisdiction is the sole responsibility of the reader and consumer.

Neither the author nor the publisher assumes any responsibility or liability whatsoever on behalf of the consumer or reader of this material. Any perceived slight of any individual or organization is purely unintentional.

The resources in this book are provided for informational purposes only and should not be used to replace the specialized training and professional judgment of a health care or mental health care professional. Neither the author nor publisher can be held responsible for the use of the information provided within this book. Please always consult a trained professional before making any decision regarding treatment of yourself or others.

Lessons from the Dojo / Peter Tocco -- 1st ed.
ISBN 978-1-7350993-0-9

As with all things, I thank God for providing me with the health, perseverance, and knowledge to share what I have learned with others. It is my sincere hope that the depth of wisdom found within the martial arts will help you as much as it has helped me.

I dedicate this book to my loving family for supporting me through difficult times, times where my strength proved wanting, and times during which I failed more often than I succeeded. Without their love and encouragement, this book would never have become a reality. I am forever grateful.

"According to all the laws of aerodynamics the bumblebee should not fly, but the bumble-bee does not know this and so flies anyway."

KUNG-FU PROVERB

氣

Your **Free** Bonus Gift

In appreciation for purchasing this book, I
am providing a **free** gift

Please use the link below to access my Author
Page where you can register to receive a free 20-
minute *Karate Sensei* Life Coaching Session

Lessons From The Dojo

www.petertoccoauthor.com

Contents

Preface

I wrote this book, for those familiar with martial arts as well as those for whom it is new, to share the wealth of knowledge and wisdom found within martial art teachings. I refer not to the art's physical skills, but the life-lessons born out of the skill and dedication of hundreds of martial art masters throughout the centuries.

All of us are familiar with some form of martial art — it pervades every facet of our media. Regrettably, what most people see, however, is a drastically watered-down version of the arts, devoid of their true purpose and meaning.

While sad, the situation is most certainly understandable because, over the last twenty-plus years, martial arts' training has evolved, or I should say, devolved, into a shadow of its former existence. In centuries past, a master selected and taught relatively few students, ensuring that each student received the necessary training to enable them to grow appreciably in mind, body, and spirit. These students generally stayed with their masters for ten or more years to acquire the requisite knowledge and skills, which they, in turn, would pass on to their students.

Today, however, the commercialization of the arts has led to a decline in both the quality of the art and the skill of the practitioner. More disappointing is the loss of the hard-earned wisdom historically passed from master to student.

Consequently, it is nearly impossible for those seeking to fully appreciate the martial arts to receive a proper education. The lack of adequate training arises from the ever-increasing number of less qualified instructors attempting to convey knowledge that they themselves do not fully understand. Also, many martial art teachings are communicated through allegory and paradox, making them difficult to learn without the benefit of informed translation. In other words, a complete understanding of martial arts is difficult without a knowledgeable sensei (teacher) to provide guidance.

The good news is that I can assist you on your journey to understand and benefit from the wisdom contained within the martial arts. Benefits I might add, that can help you in every aspect of your life, including learning how to manage challenging situations better, how to acquire a more informed, healthy perspective, and how to control emotions regarding fear, conflict, and self-doubt more effectively. I am apt to say, "You can't know what you don't know," but having trained with many authentic masters throughout my forty plus year journey, I have the experience, and I believe the obligation, to share with you what I have learned.

Albert Einstein that states, "Insanity is doing the same thing over and over again and expecting different results." In its purest sense, this book is about wisdom. Wisdom gained through the trials and tribulations of the great martial artists who have embraced the arts as a means to continually improve themselves and their students. If you choose, you may benefit from the lessons contained within this book.

If you have ever lamented over mismanaged situations, or over times when your mental and emotional discipline was found wanting, this book is an excellent tool to help improve your performance, and thereby, your quality of life. I can state this with absolute conviction because human behavior is as predictable now as it was centuries ago.

Einstein also said, "The only source of knowledge is experience," so why not benefit from the experience of the martial art pioneers that have successfully faced and overcome many of our shared challenges and done so under extremely trying circumstances? **Remember, knowledge alone is not power. Applied knowledge is power,** so consider this book an asset to unleash your potential so you can become more than the sum of your parts.

Eye of the Beholder

"How is it that you do not?" – Master Po

You may be surprised to learn that communicating martial art wisdom is more difficult that one might suspect. As stated in the preface, it involves many allegorical and paradoxical communication methods. However, I suspect that you would not be surprised to learn that one of the main tenants of the martial arts is continual self-assessment of one's strengths and weaknesses. With that in mind, to most effectively communicate the message contained within this chapter, I humbly assessed my literary strengths and weaknesses, and, finding myself lacking, I drew upon the teachings of the masters to help me achieve my goal.

Allow me to share a scene synopsis from the *Kung Fu* TV series, which aired from 1972-1975; it contained many lessons and insights into martial arts training. The scene takes place within the Shaolin Monastery, where we see a young boy, a kung-fu acolyte, sweeping the floor. Nearby, a blind elderly kung fu master, Master Po, stands serenely enjoying the peacefulness of the garden. Upon hearing the boy, he summons the boy to him, and they begin to talk. The boy, noticing that the master is blind, says, "That of all things, to live in darkness must be the worst."

The master replies, "Fear is the only darkness."

The master then tells the boy to strike him with his broom. The boy reluctantly does so, and with each attempt, the master easily redirects the boy's attack throwing him gently to the floor. The master then conveys the meaning behind the lesson by stating, "Never assume that just because a man has no eyes he cannot see."

Not through with the lesson, the master further instructs the boy to stand still and to close his eyes. He then asks the boy to tell him what he hears. The boy replies, "I hear the water; I hear the birds."

The master then asks, "Do you hear your own heartbeat?"

To which the boy replies, "No."

The master further asks, "Do you hear the grasshopper at your feet?"

The boy then opens his eyes, looks down and sees a grasshopper at his feet. The boy asks the master, "Old man, how is it that you see these things?"

The master then replies, "Young man, how is it that you do not?"

The answer to that question is the very essence of this book. Its purpose is to provide insight into key aspects of martial arts teachings so you may gain wisdom about things of which you may presently be unaware. I hope that by reading this book, you will become more like Master Po, not the acolyte.

Takeaway: Unless we open our minds to new ideas and concede that our perspective may not always be reflective of reality, we may find ourselves in situations where, as Joseph Campbell says, "the greatest tragedy in life is not so much failure but rather climbing the ladder of success and finding out that it is up against the wrong wall.

Martial Arts: Relevant Today?

"Talent hits a target no one else can hit; genius hits a target no one else can see."– Arthur Schopenhauer

It goes without saying that when trip planning, we cannot reach our destination without knowing both the starting and ending points. Simply stated, we cannot arrive *there* without knowing where *here* is.

This concept is particularly relevant to the transmission of martial art knowledge, where students often display little patience in arriving at their destination — acquiring their black belt, mastering powerful techniques, etc. Instead of working to acquire the requisite understanding of the history and purpose of the martial arts, these quick-fix practitioners invariably fall short of their goal.

Stated differently, they have failed to create a foundation for success, and instead, have built themselves a house of cards. Therefore, when training others in the arts, it is essential to provide students with the *here* to give them the best chance of reaching their destination.

It is commonly held that the formal pursuit of martial arts began centuries ago in India, and then spread slowly across the Asian continent, making its way to China, Okinawa, and ultimately, to mainland Japan. I imagine that many of us have seen movies depicting warrior monks training in Chinese monasteries such as Shaolin Temple, where they practiced kung-fu under the most trying of circumstances to perfect what we would now consider superhuman physical and mental capabilities.

We are also likely familiar with the feudal era Japan, where samurai warriors pledged allegiance to their lords and willingly sacrificed their lives in acts of extreme fidelity and courage. Their mental discipline and physical skills were legendary; they were able to master their emotions and thereby perform flawlessly, without hesitation, and without the fear and self-doubt that would have resulted in certain death. In short, their ability to acquire these skills was essential to their survival.

It would be pure idiocy for us to disregard the lessons that thousands of martial artists fought so hard to acquire. Ask yourself, is the boardroom more challenging than the battlefield? Is managing unruly children or disgruntled employees more difficult than handling insurgent troops? Can the pressure of achieving performance quotas and adhering to strict timelines be more difficult than making life or death decisions? The answer, of course, is no. Our issues generally pale in comparison. Thus, ignoring an opportunity to acquire this knowledge, knowledge we can utilize with friends and adversaries alike, would be extremely shortsighted.

It is also worth noting that the skills these early warriors and martial artists learned were not only valued on the battlefield, nor despite their origin, did they pertain solely to conflict. In fact, many of the early martial artist masters were highly regarded by their communities because of their ability to remain calm under pressure, to exhibit sound judgment, and for their ability to govern wisely, decisively, and compassionately. In short, they were pillars of poise, strength, and fairness, ensuring theirs was a just and lawful society. These individuals, through their intense training, developed the confidence and strength of character that enabled them to deal with foreign oppressors, civil and criminal disobedience, and every type of interpersonal conflict.

These masters shared martial skills with their students, as well as philosophy about handling diverse situations. Students were taught how to deal with fear, self-doubt, and conflict. These masters were teachers of men that ran the gamut of humanity. Consequently, they needed to be wise about all human interactions, not just those pertaining to martial conflict.

I provide this background to highlight that the wisdom of the martial arts was forged on the toughest of battlegrounds and across every facet of society. The early masters were adept at avoiding and managing situations with poise and an unwavering belief in individual responsibility and accountability - core principles that were effectively codified into the tenants of the martial arts. These tenants governed how a martial artist should view life, act, and make informed decisions without the emotional bias that so often produces negative results.

Hopefully, this brief background has provided you with a better understanding of and a deeper appreciation for what martial art masters have to offer. All you need do to avail yourself of this knowledge is to keep an open mind, apply what you learn, and let me guide you to a more thoughtful, peaceful, and more situationally aware existence. The following story might prove helpful in your journey.

A young boy approaches a famous master and tells him, "I wish to become your student and become the greatest martial artist in the land. How long must I study?"

"Ten years," replies the master.

"What if I study twice as hard as your other students?" asked the boy.

"Twenty years," replied the master.

"Twenty years! What if I practiced day and night?" asked the boy.

"Thirty years," replied the master.

"How is it that each time I say I will work harder, you tell me it will take longer?" the boy asked.

"The answer is clear. When one eye is fixed upon your destination, there is only one eye left with which to find the way."

The moral of the passage is that to benefit from the lessons contained in this book, you must be willing to open your mind to new and non-conventional ways of thinking. You must be able to suspend your beliefs regarding that which you think you know so that you can open yourself to new knowledge.

Takeaway: The martial arts provide a treasure trove of beneficial information. We can choose to embrace it or reject it. However, realize that rejecting it means maintaining the status quo. The wisdom within these teaching is no less relevant today then that it was centuries ago. Times change, human behavior does not.

Chapter III

Principle vs. Technique

"Pray not for a calm sea, but for a strong boat." - Unknown

Prioritizing is an essential yet apparently elusive skill. Many of us struggle with making decisions based on common sense. As the expression goes, "Common sense is not all that common." Regrettably, our collective inability to take the proper action at the proper time is often a cause of distress; our missteps lead us to rely on *hope* as a strategy. Spoiler alert, hope is not a strategy, at least not a prudent one.

So why do we fall prey to poor decision making? The reason is that many of us have a fundamental misunderstanding regarding the difference between strategy and tactics. Strategy is derivative of the core principles, concepts, and teachings that drive goal attainment. Techniques, on the other hand, are the specific actions used to implement the strategy.

In my experience, many of us rely on techniques and simply pray for a calm sea. In some cases, this decision arises from pure cognitive laziness, but quite often, it is due to misguided prioritization. Remember, we need to identify where *here* is before we can arrive at our destination, we need to ascertain the correct starting point if we want success.

For example, if I offered you the choice between learning an effective technique, be it combat-related, interpersonal, professional, etc., or of learning the principles behind the technique, which would you choose? If you opted for technique over principle, you've effectively placed the cart before the horse, which is often not the most successful strategy. That form follows function is a well-established doctrine.

Consider the following martial art example. A student attends class hoping to learn how to perform a basic kick. I agree to teach him and show him the four required steps. Several days later, I ask the student to perform the technique on a kicking shield held by another individual. When he strikes the shield, he, not the shield's holder, is forced backward. Why? Because I imprudently taught the technique before the principle.

What I should have done before teaching the student how to execute the kick, is explain to him the fundamental principle of aligning the shoulders and hips so that the kicker does not inadvertently lean away from the kick, thereby reducing power and compromising balance. Additionally, I should have incorporated the principles of body-mechanics and placed the student in the proper fighting stance with his knees slightly bent to enhance balance and to permit the non-kicking leg to root itself to the floor to derive more power. Techniques executed without a proper understanding of the fundamental principles are recipes for disaster.

This lesson — placing principle before technique — applies to every facet of learning. Take, for example, a Wall Street trader who wants to buy stock options. I can teach the individual how to execute the trade, the period in which to do it, the funds needed to transact. However, unless I teach the fundamental principles of how and why to use the options, I have not truly educated the individual. I have simply shown him or her a technique, but not provided the principles behind it.

I could provide countless examples because, quite simply, this is how we've been trained to operate in the world, desiring technique over principle. I remember a young woman once asked me how this concept could pertain to something like negotiations. I replied by asking her what she hoped to achieve. She said her goal was to obtain a larger quantity of an item at a lower price and to ensure that the other party was aware that she was someone of whom he could not take advantage.

I responded that her goal was not a principle; at best, it was a preference, perhaps even a technique, but certainly not a principle. I then provided a textbook definition of the principles involved in productive negotiations. I suggested that by better understanding these principles, she would receive greater benefit because her techniques would be in sync with her goals.

Technique flows from the principle, so in the case of negotiations, it might look something like this:

Principles:

- Create an attitude that prompts the negotiator to work for solutions that will benefit all or most of the participating parties.
- Create an orientation that views the other person as a potential partner rather than an adversary.
- Create a climate that stimulates both parties to realize that they are more likely to attain their objectives if they work together than if they battle one another.

- Create a set of goals that facilitate the process of securing mutual advantages.

Techniques:
- Separate the people from the problem - in other words, be kind to people, tough on issues.
- Focus on interests, not positions.
- Generate a variety of possibilities before deciding.
- Define objective standards as the criteria for making the decision.

Using these fundamental guidelines serves both parties by improving the probability of a conflict-free outcome while fostering mutual respect and trust.

This example highlights the importance of putting the cart after the horse. Intentional and appropriate use of principles and techniques are effective practices, whether on the battlefield or in the boardroom. Remember, excellent techniques derive from sound principles. Anything less is just a roll of the dice.

Takeaway: Principle drives technique, form follows function. Identify the principles and the techniques will support the principals naturally and efficiently.

Chapter IV

Constant in the Equation

"We do not rise to the level of our expectations. We fall to the level of our training." – Unknown

Most of us would agree that solving equations with more variables than constants is a challenging prospect. Yet, we often find ourselves in these situations, resulting in unmet expectations, stress, frustration, and a healthy dose of personal disappointment — all of which negatively impact our self-confidence and prevent us from reaching our potential.

How, then, do we alleviate these challenging situations to achieve our goals? How do we increase our chances of driving forward in the face of adversity and seemingly insurmountable problems while making informed decisions and responding effectively? The answer: *You* must become the constant in the equation!

I have seen many martial art examples where clearly one of the participants was in total control, not necessarily because of that individual's physical prowess, but because of that person's intrinsic self-knowledge, self-awareness, and self-confidence. Further, I have witnessed many matches involving true masters of their art, many of whom were more than sixty years of age, effortlessly defeat younger, stronger, and more physically fit opponents. In several instances, the master was simultaneously sparring with multiple opponents! To me, it appeared as if the opponents were attacking in slow motion, and that the master was anticipating his opponent's attacks as if they were choreographed beforehand. I have experienced such encounters, and I can assure you this phenomenon is both real and humbling.

Making sense of this phenomenon begs the question, "How can one individual so completely control an encounter containing so many opponents?" The answer lies in one's training. More specifically, in one's ability to train in such a way that they transcend technique, embody principles, and become one with their art. *Effortless effort* is a term often used to describe a person so in tune with his or her being - mind, body, and spirit - that to the uninitiated, action looks completely effortless. To achieve this degree of martial arts mastery, students must train for years to perfect their physical technique and mental discipline, so that in time of need, the practitioner and the technique are one.

When this happens, actions are no longer directed by conscious thought. Instead, the unconscious mind drives the body resulting in quicker, more precise, and more intuitive action. Conversely, when action is directed by conscious thought, as it is with a novice, the movement is more reactive than intuitive because the mind filters our actions and slows our response.

Those who have achieved mastery act without conscious thought, thereby making their movements incredibly quick, powerful, and natural. To the uninitiated, it looks as if the masters know what their opponents are attempting well in advance of the actual attack. Not true. The masters simply see things as they truly are without the bias of conscious thought. Achieving this level of mental acuity and technical proficiency enables the practitioner to become the constant in the equation.

Like the masters, we, too, can transform ourselves and dramatically increase the likelihood of achieving successful outcomes. Moreover, we can apply this principle to every facet of our lives. Once we successfully incorporate these principles into one aspect of our life, it becomes easier to apply them throughout other parts of our lives. I have used this principle in numerous personal and professional settings ranging from high risk, anxiety-producing situations as a federal law enforcement officer, to high-stakes Wall Street trading decisions, to board room negotiations.

The key to becoming the constant in the equation lies in the ability to control your anxiety and your fear of the unknown. These emotions tax our conscious mind to the point where they impede performance. They erode confidence, which fuels the fire of insecurity, and in turn, clouds our conscious mind. This does not need to be our reality.

Consider the following. I began studying karate as a young, slight of stature, anxiety-filled nine-year-old. I did not choose to study karate; instead, it was forced upon me by my parents. After accepting my fate, I quickly realized that everyone in the school had the same tools with which to work—two arms, two legs, and one brain. It sounds simple, but that revelation eliminated a great deal of anxiety because I realized that I was on an ostensibly level playing field. This awareness was a critical breakthrough.

Finding commonalities in situations allows us to better relate to the situation, significantly reducing our anxiety while building our confidence; these are two essential components to becoming the constant in the equation.

As my training progressed and I performed countless repetitions of the drills, I identified additional similarities between my classmates and me; we all hated the drills, and everyone was exhausted, sore, and frustrated after training. Over time, I began to see that there were more similarities than differences among us.

When multiple-opponent fighting was introduced, my anxiety again spiked. Several months later, the anxiety dissipated as I became more familiar with the drill, and therefore better able to perform naturally. I no longer needed to consciously direct my body to act, because my unconscious mind, with the familiarity and confidence that comes from endless hours of practice, knew exactly how to respond. I had successfully transformed myself into a constant by eliminating the variables of anxiety and fear by identifying the commonalities in the situation.

Becoming the constant in the equation requires:

1. **Identifying similarities in situations.**

Anxiety and fear limit performance by focusing the conscious mind on inconsequential matters. Freedom of thought and action derive from the unconscious mind, which is set free when anxiety and fear are reduced.

Total removal of anxiety is not necessary if we can alleviate the burden on our conscious mind. Like a computer, when we expend our processing power on non-essential applications, it diminishes our performance. To achieve our goal, therefore, we must first direct our efforts toward identifying the similarities in the situation.

2. **Continuous execution of proper techniques.**
He who fails to plan, plans to fail. Preparation is the key to any successful endeavor. You cannot expect your body and mind to perform appropriately if you do not provide the proper input. The input must be relevant to the goal and diligently performed, or you will experience a garbage in, garbage out result. The adage "practice makes perfect," is inaccurate; a more accurate statement is "perfect practice makes perfect," so you must practice diligently and with precision.

Whatever your goal, you can train yourself to become proficient to the point of becoming the constant in the equation. Press secretaries, for example, continuously practice the best way to field difficult and unexpected questions. Special Forces soldiers drill incessantly on how to respond to fluid combat situations. Regardless of the thing you try to master, you simply need to find the right element to train, and results will surely follow.

In summary, if you seek to improve your performance, you must remove fear and doubt from the equation. Become as familiar as possible with the situation. Think about the first time you did anything challenging, and then think about when you did that same action the next time. Did you really become that much more proficient in that second instance, or did you become more familiar and, therefore, less anxious, fearful, and self-doubting?

To become truly proficient, you must perform numerous repetitions of the desired action/behavior, until the body and mind know the subject matter on an unconscious level, thereby allowing your mind to perform naturally and intuitively. These steps are synergistic, not sequential. Repetition brings familiarity, which reduces anxiety. Identifying similarities brings comfort, which allows you to work more productively.

Takeaway: Becoming the constant in the equation is the key to enhancing your personal and professional life. Start small, master one task or situation where you can truly become the constant in the equation. Then expand and repeat.

Chapter V

Defining Defeat

"I have not failed. I've just found 10,000 ways that won't work."– Thomas Edison

Many of us have a binary world view in which we perceive situations as being either positive or negative, or successful or unsuccessful. In other words, we often have a perspective where the is little or no middle ground, where everything is, instead, viewed in absolute terms.

I believe most of us would say that this is an unhealthy and limiting perspective, one that may lead to a negative mindset of failure, low self-worth, and a belief that life is negative and unchangeable. To be honest, many martial artists also have a binary world view, except ours is one which rejects the negative in absolute terms.

The essential difference is that martial artists believe negative is not actually negative. It is not either good or bad; it is instead good or better. This mindset views obstacles as objectives, as opportunities for growth. In this way, we can pull victory from defeat by extracting that which we find beneficial.

Everything we perceive is subjective because we can only process situations based upon our respective experiences and training. Yes, two plus two equals four. This equation is an objective law of nature, but perceptions are constructs of our minds, and therefore subjective. We each define our reality. By changing the premise that outcomes are either positive or negative, we change the paradigm. Shifting our point of view sounds simple, but because we are creatures of habit and subject to the laws of science, mindset change will not arise without directed effort. We must create this positive mind/body perspective.

I believe in the idiom, "We are as happy as we allow ourselves to be." But extracting the positive from a negative is far from easy, though certainly not impossible. As human beings, our minds forge neural pathways that, with repeated use, reinforce our existing thought patterns - positive or negative. Cognitive

Behavioral Therapy (CBT) and Dialectical Behavior Therapy (DBT) are used to help people change their thought patterns and behavior, and to learn to live in the moment to manage stress more effectively.

Knowing that the martial arts are a microcosm of the world, many martial art masters strive to provide students with mindset changing tools that help them perceive the world in a way more conducive to their development. In truth, an inability to move away from negative thinking and emotions was detrimental to the warrior's existence. Limiting their mindset to view only good or bad prevented them from learning from their mistakes, a skill essential to their survival.

The encouraging news is that with practice, we can change our thinking. The first step is recognizing the challenge. The second step is encouraging ourselves to look at past and current obstacles and try to identify the positives in these situations. By doing so, we learn valuable lessons we can utilize going forward. Warriors on the battle did not consider losing synonymous with defeat. Defeat was reserved for those that either did not try or those that did not learn from the situation.

Bringing the lesson forward, we can see how something as harmless as a sporting competition, which on its surface is healthy and natural, can, for those with low self-esteem and a narrow view of victory and defeat, be an incredibly stressful and potentially destructive experience. For these individuals, seeing the glass half full and embracing the concept of achieving a moral victory after a physical defeat are non-existent. Instead, they view their inability to achieve the desired result only as a negative.

This tragic and debilitating mindset is prevalent among today's youth. It is preventable, however, and the cure lies not in changing the rules of competition, but in changing one's perception of what constitutes victory and defeat. I contend that we can significantly improve the quality of our lives simply by changing the way we define these concepts.

When I was a child and just beginning my training, my school attended dozens of karate tournaments each year; opting out was not an option, I was required to compete. I competed and soon realized that I was an anxiety-filled student with little self-confidence and an unassertive nature. Consequently, I competed in dozens of tournaments and almost always walked away demoralized and empty-handed. At the time, I viewed my inability to win as a complete failure. I saw nothing redeeming in my defeats, and I grew increasingly resentful of other's success.

One fateful day, however, things changed for the better. I was entered in the teenage, black belt division at a major tournament that attracted top martial artists from across the region. As fate would have it, my randomly drawn opponent was the previous year's champion. He had all sorts of patches and adornments on his karate uniform, indications of his achieved victories and advanced rank.

I was a newly minted black belt who, while gaining confidence in my abilities, was still unable to get negativity and fear of defeat out of my mind. Part of this fear was because my training was not geared toward tournament competition, but instead, was focused on real-world self-defense. Consequently, I was not schooled in the tricks of the trade often utilized while playing the tournament competition game.

Before the match, my instructor called me over and told me that the reason I had not won many matches was that I was trying to play a game, tournament karate, with which I was unfamiliar. He advised me to forget about trying to score points and suggested I fight using the aggressive style we employ in our home dojo. In other words, I was directed to fight hard and establish physical dominance and not to be concerned with scoring points.

This advice changed my whole perspective regarding the upcoming match, and it also provided tangential benefits that I presently retain. My opponent and I bowed to each other to start the match. I had no idea if I would be victorious, but neither did I have any doubt about my ability to perform as my sensei had advised.

For the first time ever, I had no concern about winning or losing. I also knew that my opponent was not prepared for what was to come. I am proud to say that I manhandled the east coast champion to the point that the match had to be stopped twice.

In the end, I lost the match on points, but I could not have been happier, and our resident champion could not have been more shaken. It was a decisive turning point for me, and it happened exactly when it was supposed to happen. We cannot rush change, but we must be prepared for it when it presents itself. It was my time to change. It was time for my thinking to evolve, which brings to mind another great quote,

> "When the student is ready, the Master appears." – Buddhist Proverb

In the eyes of many, I had accomplished something special that day. I had done what no one else had previously been able to do, so what some may perceive as defeat was nothing of the sort. In hindsight, it was my first experience with the concept of a Pyrrhic victory - a victory not worth winning because much was lost achieving it—which is no doubt what my opponent experienced. It was my first conscious experience with winning despite not being victorious. It was an eye-opening experience, and one I hope will resonate with those who may suffer from having a narrow view of victory and defeat.

From that day on, win or lose, I never suffered defeat or experienced failure again, because those conditions occur only when you don't put in your best effort, or when you neglect to learn from the experience. Presently, I make it a point to learn from every experience, personal or professional, and by doing so, I ensure that while I might not always be victorious, I will never experience failure and defeat.

Takeaway: The key to consistently winning lies in redefining our perception of victory and defeat. Viewing stumbling blocks as stepping-stones to continual growth and self-awareness is the surest way to achieve outcome-independent success.

Preparedness

"The trouble with the future is that it usually arrives before we are ready for it." – Arnold H. Glasow

As a former law enforcement professional and longtime martial artist, I am prepared to deal with most combat-related threats. But, like many of us, my situational awareness is strongest in situations with which I am most familiar. This is a common trait among us, and one I hope the following example will illustrate.

In addition to writing, I have a passion for teaching martial arts and self-defense courses. My favorite course to teach is *Situational Awareness Training* (SAT). The goal of the course is to educate participants regarding the things they do or fail to do, that make them more or less likely to become a victim. One of the key points I emphasize is that "Crimes of Opportunity" occur because WE provide the opportunity!"

When it comes to safety, all of us could benefit from being more aware. No one is immune from becoming a target; this applies to all types of attacks, physical, emotional, personal, professional, and so on. SAT is a PowerPoint-driven course—which you can reference at the end of this book—that teaches participants personal defense best practices they can use to become freer, safer, and more confident.

During the presentation, I highlight two slides that illustrate how, based upon our respective backgrounds, we are situationally aware more often in some environments than others. The goal is to help participants realize how much they may be neglecting regarding their self-defense practices. This course helps participants recognize that by opening their eyes to different ways of viewing situations, they can, in a few hours, acquire an enhanced situational awareness capability.

One slide shows a picture of a woman's black high heel shoes with a bright red sole. After showing the slide, I ask only the men to describe everything they can about what they see. I usually receive very generic replies like I see shiny, black high-heel shoes that look hard to walk in.

When I ask the women in the group for their comments, they are not surprisingly much more specific and descriptive. For example, comments would include, they are last years' Christian Louboutin, patent leather, 4-inch stilettos.

I then show a photo of several men playing basketball, where we see one of the men at the forefront shooting a basket. I ask the women what they see. Typical responses include a close-up of a man shooting a basketball in a gym with others doing the same standing further away. With the men, I receive more precise details such as, based on the uniforms, it was a practice session, not a game, and the person shooting the ball is taking a 3-point shot.

So, what does this have to do with preparedness? Everything, because when you increase your situational awareness regarding things about which you were previously unaware, you will inevitably become better prepared to manage the situation. The early karate masters appreciated the need to be prepared, and to anticipate problematic situations, even those that were unlikely. Remember, the masters focused their attention on the situations that might occur, rather than fixating on potential responses. Attention to a preordained response to a situation would unquestionably impede their ability to respond naturally.

Herein lies the paradox. To efficiently respond to potential events, we need to think strategically about the potential situation, not about our preordained response. Focusing on the response influences our performance. This, in turn, inhibits the free-flowing reaction that occurs naturally when we're connected to our intuition.

I once asked a business colleague how he always seems prepared when meeting with clients or superiors. His answer influences my thinking to this day. Essentially, he told me that he goes into each board meeting expecting to be fired or to be promoted, to be praised or to be reprimanded. He expects his usual seat will be taken, and that whatever time he was supposed to speak, and whatever topic he was to speak about, would be different from what was initially scheduled. I suggested that approach might be a bit time consuming and excessive. He replied, "It just takes a little practice, but the rewards are well worth it." Today I agree.

This dialogue highlights the concept of anticipating potential scenarios so that you can adopt a strategy of preparedness without designing a prearranged response. At the same time, this strategy allows you to maintain the calm assurance of knowing that you will rarely be caught off guard. The response or technique you employ after that arises from your training and your ever-improving interpersonal skills.

I will offer one final example, a personal favorite because it involves my father, who served several years in the Navy before spending 32 years as a New York City Police Officer. As a child, I loved to hide in various places around our house and wait for him to walk by so I could jump out and try to scare him. I thought it was fun, and he did not seem to mind, so it became a regular occurrence. I cannot remember a single instance when he reacted anxiously. I never heard a startled yell or saw a fear-based response. In short, it was as if he always expected something to happen.

I eventually asked him why I had never caught him off guard, and he replied that he generally maintained a state of acute situational awareness, rarely letting his mind get too preoccupied with any particular thought. This mindset is easier to talk about than practice, I admit, but nonetheless possible and beneficial, to say the least.

Takeaway: Anticipating future events is an essential part of being prepared. However, we tend to go awry when we decide a response in advance of the situation. Thinking strategically about potential events is prudent. Yet we must trust our instincts because we cannot defend against an attack with a strategy designed for a different attack. If we train properly, our skills will ensure we respond appropriately.

Chapter VII

Strategy & Tactics

"Strategy without tactics is the slowest route to victory. Tactics without strategy is the noise before defeat."
— Sun Tzu

For many of us, the thought of changing tactics, particularly in mid-stream, is unfathomable. We need look no further than to our own Revolutionary and Civil Wars, where soldiers from both sides, defying all present-day logic, simply marched in straight rows firing at each other until one side was victorious. This tactic, mind you, was employed by some of the greatest generals of the time: George Washington, Ulysses S Grant, Robert E. Lee, to name a few.

These intelligent and well-trained men were so caught up in employing known, yet ineffective tactics, that thousands upon thousands of soldiers died that might otherwise have lived. The concept of guerrilla warfare changed this paradigm, but that provides little solace for the families of those needlessly lost.

People cite numerous reasons for clinging to their current practices, arguing that the risk of change is not worth the reward. Expressions like, "If it ain't broke, don't fix it," or, "You can't teach an old dog new tricks," exemplify this limiting mindset. While some arguments may have merit, most do not pass muster, and moreover, they severely limit a person's ability to achieve a successful outcome. In short, they are convenient excuses to engage in familiar behavior and thereby maintain the status quo.

If we accept the maxim that form follows function, we should also accept that function is based on need, not preference. This means that one should not tailor a tactical approach, based upon personal preferences or comfort level, but rather upon the needs of the situation, the strategic goal. For example, while a fly swatter is light and flexible, it is the wrong tool with which to bang nails. Similarly, while a hammer might be a 6-year old's choice to whack bugs, most would hopefully disagree.

We go astray when we let our comfort level and preferences dictate our tactics. I once heard the expression, "The comfort zone is a great place to visit, but nothing grows there." I wholeheartedly agree with the sentiment, and I believe even the best strategy will fail unless the tactics are sound and aligned with achieving the goal. In short, they must be appropriately tailored to the specific situation.

Think for a minute of individuals that you know who, regardless of the situation, use the same tactics. This is absurd. It seems that for these people, the concept of aligning the tactics with strategy is foreign. Take, for example, individuals with aggressive personalities that try to dominate a situation by sheer will of force; they have no awareness that the circumstances may require a less aggressive, more diplomatic approach. A one-size-fits-all approach derived from personal preference or comfort level makes a successful outcome unlikely. Success occurs when strategy and tactics are in sync.

Early in my training, I repeatedly used my favorite technique regardless of the situation. My decision was based partly upon prior success, but mostly upon the comfort level I felt when using the familiar move. If I had more judiciously chosen my techniques, I would unquestionably have been more successful. Instead, I continually relied upon a familiar yet imprudent approach, disregarding the needs of the situation. In effect, I took a strength and turned it into a weakness; I became predictable because my tactics remained the same despite the circumstances.

In my opinion, knowing when to forgo the familiar — when to change tactics—is more art than science. It is, however, the key to maximizing potential and avoiding problems. Adherence to the familiar makes you predictable. Predictability makes you easier to defeat in battle and in life. As we have learned, knowing oneself and one's opponent is the surest way to victory. When your adversary is expecting X, move outside your comfort zone, and deliver Y.

It is human nature to categorize people into groups based upon perception. Labeling others as assertive, lazy, weak, or ignorant is something we do both consciously and unconsciously. Whether friend or foe, we continuously evaluate others' behavior, and they ours, to determine how we should interact. What this implies is that your ability to achieve goals and to be treated appropriately is irrevocably linked to your ability to sync your tactics with your strategy, whether in the boardroom, the classroom, the living room, or in combat.

Takeaway: Continuous repetition of familiar behavior makes you easier to anticipate, manipulate, and defeat — it makes you vulnerable. Whether the attack is premeditated or spontaneous, physical or emotional, failing to vary your response will reduce your odds of success. Adapt your actions to the needs of the situation. Stray outside your comfort zone to keep others off balance, and remember, as Vince Lombardi, one of the most revered professional football coaches, once said, "Hope is not a strategy."

Chapter VIII

Conquering Anger

"The angry man will defeat himself in battle as well as in life."– Samurai Maxim

"You will not be punished for your anger; you will be punished by your anger."– Buddha

Because controlling anger is a big challenge for me, I decided that two quotes would be appropriate for this subject. That said, both speak to virtually the same point. Our anger generally does not serve us well. Reflecting on poor decisions I have made, I confess that I made many of them while angry.

I have heard it said that anger is a secondary emotion, the byproduct of another primary sentiment: frustration, indignance, jealously, etc. Because of this, we must be particularly mindful of what factors and character traits drive us to a state of anger. All of us experience these emotions. We can, however, take what is unique about us and use it to better control our responses.

Throughout the years, I have seen martial art masters control opponents and situations like a conductor leading an orchestra. To me, the amount of physical skill they exhibited was genuinely remarkable. But the most impressive skill I observed was their noteworthy self-control. Their ability to control fear, anger, and disappointment was astounding. I found their self-control particularly notable because I must continually work on my restraint.

One day, after witnessing an example of this remarkable self-control, I approached the karate master to question him about his ability to remain calm and to refrain from taking physical action. He replied, "Choosing not to act is an act in itself, and it is far easier to strike another than to refrain from striking. I refrain from aggressive behavior not for the benefit of my adversary, but as a continuing test of my character and control."

These words resonated with me because I had, for so long, sought yet failed to control my temper. I saw my aggressive outbursts as the byproduct of righteous indignation, something I was justified to feel and empowered to act upon. This conversation, however, significantly changed my viewpoint. By seeing anger and its manifestations as a test of my skill and self-control, I now viewed controlling this emotion as a worthy challenge. I saw it as an opportunity for personal growth—as a way to not let anger defeat me by dictating my actions.

Managing anger is an essential part of an effective self-defense mechanism because it helps us think clearly and thus make rational decisions. The early masters realized that in combat, anger served only to cloud the mind, causing one to expend needless energy and to become tense when one needed to be calm. For them, it was a recipe for defeat, and defeat usually meant death. Therefore, the masters attempted to treat their emotions as if they were nothing more than passing thoughts not to be engaged.

Consequently, they manifested the clarity of thought needed to be entirely in the moment and achieve oneness of mind and body. Eventually, this philosophy transcended all aspects of their lives and resulted in the early masters becoming well-respected community leaders as well as masters of their respective arts. And, in my experience, mastering this aspect of my life has provided considerable carry-over benefits into other parts of my life. I am confident the same will be true for you. The samurai maxim I feel that best exemplifies this point is, "A man who has attained mastery of an art reveals it in every action."

Takeaway: Anger is a secondary, byproduct, emotion in response to a primary emotion. Often anger stems from a self-perceived inadequacy or character flaw within us. By seeking the source of our anger and having the courage to face its negative manifestations, we will become free from anger's hold on us, and it will no longer dictate our actions.

Analysis Paralysis

"Nothing will ever be attempted if all possible objections must first be overcome." – Samuel Johnson

Wikipedia defines analysis paralysis as a situation where the sheer quantity of analysis overwhelms the decision-making process itself, thus preventing a decision. To me, that is a long-winded way of saying analysis paralysis leads to dysfunctional decision making.

If the martial artists of old suffered from this condition, I would not have much to write about because they would have lived a short and painful life. Fortunately, these historic warriors were able to move beyond the hesitation caused by overthinking and act decisively and with conviction.

Today, there is so much noise in our heads, so much useless information floating around the internet and the news media, that it is difficult to know what to use and what to tune out to make timely, informed decisions. Indeed, many intelligent and motivated people suffer from analysis paralysis; one could argue this is the direct byproduct of our information-overload society.

Note, however, that making a conscious decision not to act is entirely different from being unable to act - analysis paralysis. Analysis paralysis is the inability to act because an individual cannot choose between and among options. To reach our potential, we need to identify ways to eliminate analysis paralysis and be cognizant of the difference between choosing not to act, and not being able to act.

In the martial arts, failure to act decisively is generally met with immediate and unfavorable results. To avoid such results, the early masters realized that prioritizing certain aspects of their training was essential to their survival. They understood that it was imprudent to attempt to master dozens of techniques; instead, prioritization led to simplicity of action. Therefore, they focused on mastering the basics, striving to become an inch wide and a mile deep, versus a mile wide and an inch deep. To avoid analysis paralysis, it is essential to prioritize decisions rather than treat them as if they all held the same importance.

After prioritizing their decisions, the masters subsequently broke them into smaller, more manageable pieces. This method helped them perfect techniques necessary to implement their strategy while also allowing them to identify flaws quickly. It is far easier to think through a component of something than to think it through in its entirety.

The opposite of analysis paralysis can best be summed up by the samurai maxim "To know and to act are one and the same." Reaching this stage of intuitive action is unquestionably difficult, but if we follow the path established by the masters, we can see that working backward from the desired outcome helps clarify the decision-making process. Therefore, by working backward from the desired outcome, by prioritizing options, and by breaking our options down into more manageable components, we can significantly increase our odds of achieving an optimal outcome.

Remember, overcoming analysis paralysis does not mean that we make instantaneous decisions as we would in combat. Instead, we benefit simply by reducing the distracting noise in our head, which in turn increases our odds of making timely, prudent decisions.

Takeaway: The key to eliminating analysis paralysis is freeing our mind so that it can perform in a natural state. We do this by identifying an acceptable yet imperfect solution, which we then break down into smaller, more manageable components. Relieved of the burden of finding the perfect solution, our unconscious mind will then be free to work on identifying more creative, intuitive solutions. The evidence is compelling. We have nothing to lose but our analysis paralysis.

Chapter X

Fear & Self-Doubt

"Control your emotions, or they will control you."
– Chinese Adage

The ancient masters understood one concept above all others. You cannot be victorious over others unless you have first achieved victory over yourself. To accomplish this, these early warriors subjected themselves to incredibly rigorous training so that not only would their bodies become strong, but their mental and emotional discipline would also develop appreciably.

This holistic approach was essential to their survival, because without self-knowledge —the unity of mind, body, and spirit —they would never have survived the perils of the time. This holistic training, with its emphasis on knowing both one's own capabilities and those of their opponents, is what kept these warriors alive. I believe this philosophy is best expressed by legendary Sun Tzu, a Chinese general, military strategist, and philosopher, who said, "If you know the enemy and know yourself, you need not fear the result of a hundred battles. If you know yourself but not the enemy, for every victory gained you will also suffer a defeat. If you know neither the enemy nor yourself, you will succumb in every battle."

Aside from the obvious martial implications, I believe the message carries the more profound meaning that if we are to have any hope of living a life free of fear, ignorance, and self-doubt, of being victorious over ourselves and others, then the journey must begin from within. Sun Tzu is stating that the external challenges we face are but half the battle, and for us to achieve real triumph, true freedom and control, the victory we seek is within us. Unless and until we control our emotions and the way we process life's inputs, we will continue to wallow in mediocrity. I believe that to be unknown to oneself is the greatest of sins and the root cause of many human failings.

How then, do we acquire the emotional control and self-knowledge that is the key to our success and the first step in our journey? Like with most martial art lessons, the solution requires us to break the problem down into smaller components. Of the three unproductive, life-draining emotions—ignorance, fear, and self-doubt — the easiest one to remedy is ignorance, for it requires only the desire to learn and to apply change.

For example, the ancient masters knew that a martial *art* was primarily a martial *science* — physics, biology, chemistry, etc. A practitioner only progressed from martial *scientist* to martial *artist* by mastering the science and making it an integral part of his or her very being. They did this by overcoming their ignorance and increasing their knowledge about bodily functions such as respiratory control, adrenal responses, etc., and by improving their understanding of body mechanics, which include the physics behind the movements. This understanding was imperative because, without a substantive knowledge of body dynamics, their battlefield capabilities would have been diminished.

The encouraging news is that because ignorance, fear, and self-doubt are linked, the byproduct of mitigating one will result in a tangential benefit to all. In this example, the ancient masters increased their knowledge about the human body, thereby removing their ignorance. Armed with this new knowledge, they gained the confidence that enabled them to overcome self-doubt. Free from self-doubt, they were able to eliminate the fear that in combat, would have assuredly resulted in death.

This sequential process of removing ignorance, self-doubt, and fear is played out daily across the spectrum of human interaction. Fortunately, these principles hold regardless of the situation, but for us to be successful, we must remain positive and believe in our pending success. Being positive provides the impetus we need to tackle our difficult, but not insurmountable challenges. We must avoid falling into the negative mindset so well stated in Mark Twain's quote, "I have had a horrible life, most of which never happened."

Unfortunately, I believe this quote sums up the way many of us think. I also believe that our society accentuates viewing things through a negative prism; many see the glass as being half empty. This negative thinking destroys our spirit, which in turn prevents us from taking the steps necessary to rid ourselves of unproductive emotions.

So, where do we begin? The first step is to simply know consistent positive thinking is possible. We have empirical evidence passed down not only from centuries of martial art masters who achieved self-mastery but from millions of ordinary people that have turned their lives around and overcome tremendous hardship. Knowing this, we can lay claim to the positive mindset that will enable us to conquer the first and most easily changeable obstacle — ignorance.

Ignorance is the primary component to address because once we have knowledge that something exists, we can develop a more thorough understanding of it. Note, however, that knowledge alone does not eliminate ignorance. This is not earth science, where merely knowing that the plants give off oxygen and that humans produce carbon dioxide is sufficient. We must apply our knowledge for it to be beneficial, particularly when dealing with the myriad of complex human emotions.

Regarding applied knowledge, consider, for example, knowing that someone can defend themselves with a punch or a kick. While informative, knowing that a punch or kick can be used for self-defense is just short of useless if you don't understand how to utilize the knowledge. To arrive at the point where our samurai maxim, "To know and to act are one and the same" becomes real, we must strive to move beyond mere knowledge and seek genuine understanding.

Takeaway: The path to reaching our potential begins with the positive belief that we can achieve the goal. This belief provides the motivation to acquire the knowledge and understanding required to rid ourselves of the ignorance, self-doubt, and fear that prevents us from reaching our potential.

Preemptive Strikes

"To be prepared for war is one of the most effectual means of preserving peace."– George Washington

Those who study martial arts are familiar with the expression "There is no first strike in karate." This expression represents the philosophical basis of the martial arts, namely that a martial artist should never initiate or escalate a confrontation. Moreover, it adheres to the tenant that martial artists should only use their skills for self-defense.

In the medical profession, doctors take a Hippocratic Oath to do no harm to their patients. Their function is to identify and treat patient illness with as little negative consequence as possible. They are not at liberty to take extreme measures or to act without patient consent. What they can do, however, is proactively assess avenues for the prevention and early detection of illnesses. By doing so, they provide an incredibly valuable service by increasing their patients' odds of achieving successful outcomes.

Regarding the martial arts, there is no established, legally binding oath requiring practitioners to use their considerable skills in a benevolent manner; there never was. Instead, the role of ensuring that practitioners embraced the principles of non-aggression was left to the masters themselves as they assessed the moral character of prospective students before accepting them. To aid in the possess, an informal code of ethics arose within the martial arts community — the most notable being the *Twenty Precepts of Shotokan Karate* established by master Gichin Funakoshi. The most famous of those precepts is "Karate ni sente nashi," meaning there is no first strike in karate.

This philosophy is often misunderstood to mean that when a martial artist perceives that a threat is real and imminent, they must wait until the attack is launched before responding. This is absurd. It leaves the individual needlessly vulnerable, particularly if the threat is significant - if weapons or multiple opponents are involved. Instead, the philosophy refers to the concept of non-instigation and non-confrontation. It is a practitioner's duty to attempt to mitigate or avoid confrontation whenever possible. That said, preemptive strikes *are* an essential part of a martial artist's self-defense capability.

For example, imagine that a person who expresses an intense dislike for you, buys a hunting knife, dresses in black, hides outside your house at night, and then sneaks up behind you as you approach your front door. Would you say this person intended you harm? Should you wait until the knife is inches away before acting? Of course not, you should and would take preemptive action. The philosophy of non-aggression and tolerance is not designed to increase one's odds of becoming a victim.

So, what is the relevance of this philosophy today? The answer is found in the principle known as the preemptive strike. Consider how many of us, in our daily interaction with others, get caught off guard, and find ourselves less than adequately prepared for whatever situation we encounter - an encounter no less, that we surely believed was forthcoming. Too many it seems, refrain from taking preemptive action for fear of being considered overly aggressive, or because we are uncomfortable initiating confrontation. Remember, confrontation is just another form of communication, but communication need not be confrontational; we have the power to change the outcome of the encounter.

Note that when we fail to act preemptively, we unknowingly increase the likelihood that we will experience the very physical, emotional, or psychological confrontation that we were trying to avoid. Emboldened by what is observed as passive behavior, adversaries seek to exploit the perceived weakness, whether in the classroom, the board room, or anywhere the opportunity presents itself.

Therefore, preemptive strikes are not only incredibly beneficial but unquestionably related to the doctrine, there is no first strike in karate. By taking preemptive action, we have more control over the outcome, because we, not they, will be setting the tone and tenor of the discussion.

Imagine that a tenant pays the rent late every month, and the landlord fails to take remedial action. The landlord, knowingly or not, is creating a potentially problematic and likely perpetual situation. Similarly, if we fail to address work situations where we may have been incorrectly assigned blame, we may again be creating a potentially problematic and perpetual situation. Patterns of abusive behavior are quickly established because they provide the actor with a great sense of power and control.

Conversely, if we initiate a preemptive strike to address matters on our terms (time, location, etc.) before they evolve into detrimental patterns, we send notice that we are willing to defend ourselves. Therefore, before the landlord accepts a past due rent check, he or she should approach the tenant preemptively and address the matter before it becomes problematic.

Similarly, before we are faced with a post-incident confrontation with our manager, we might consider communicating in advance that while we are always willing to take responsibility for our actions, we do not feel that the situation was handled appropriately. Done correctly, we can reasonably expect that the situation will change for the better because we have controlled the encounter with a preemptive strike, and by doing so, set the stage for future encounters

Takeaway: Demonstrating the willingness to take preemptive action mitigate acts designed to injure, embarrass, sabotage, and otherwise harm us, whether at the PTA or in the boardroom. Preemptive action is self-defense. It is not random, uncontrolled, and aggressive behavior. Moreover, even a single demonstration of this capability will communicate our message to potential adversaries.

Chapter XII

Change vs. Transition

"Change is situational. Transition, on the other hand, is psychological. It is not those events, but rather the inner reorientation or self-redefinition that you have to go through in order to incorporate any of those changes into your life. Without a transition, a change is just a rearrangement of the furniture." – William Bridges

When I began training in the art of karate, I often wondered how martial artists like Bruce Lee and Chuck Norris performed at levels so far beyond that of their contemporaries. At the time, I assumed that they were fortunate enough to have received exceptional God-given abilities - that they were members of life's exceptional gene pool.

This belief lasted until I began watching their training. What I observed was nothing short of amazing, and it had a profound effect on my approach to training and preparation. Their training regimes reflected the old warrior mantra that states, "If you fail to train, you just trained to fail. The more you sweat in training, the less you bleed in battle." This mantra captures the true essence of martial art training - disciplined preparation and exceptional effort.

If you need more proof of proper training's value and ability to help individuals overcome significant obstacles, consider this, Bruce Lee was 5' 8", weighed less than 130 pounds, and one leg was nearly an inch shorter than the other. He wore contact lenses, and he failed a 1963 physical exam, which excluded him from the U.S. Army draft. Additionally, he suffered a severe spinal injury and was told that he might never walk again. Contrast these facts with my initial belief that Bruce Lee's capabilities were derived from superior genetics.

Why is this relevant? Think back to earlier chapters where I highlighted stories about elderly masters effortlessly dominating younger, more vigorous opponents. Although these masters spent countless hours acquiring and mastering their techniques, which in the above quote would equate to *making changes*, this was not the sole source of their success. They also understood the wisdom of studying the psychological aspects of the art, which in the above quote would equate to *making transitions*. The combination of physical and mental awareness and training is what led to success. Indeed, without intrinsically linking physical change to a corresponding transition in mindset, they would merely have been rearranging the furniture.

Change is simply an action, while transition is a psychological mindset that facilitates growth and allows us to reach our potential. In your own life, consider a situation where you can change your actions and transition your thinking. This combination will help you achieve permanent, beneficial results.

This truth has been borne out by centuries of martial artists facing the most trying circumstances imaginable, and additionally, by everyday people who similarly embrace martial art teachings. Our goal, therefore, should not be simply to change, but instead, to transition so that the actor and the actions are inexorably linked.

Takeaway: When facing situations, our goal should be to respond, not react. This is only possible with the mind / body unity that comes when we embrace transition.

Chapter XIII

Tai Sabaki

"Never mistake motion for action." – Ernest Hemingway

As a young martial artist, I vividly remember watching Aikido masters swirl around the dojo floor, effortlessly avoiding the punches and kicks thrown at them by accomplished martial artists. Amazed, I wondered how these masters could, with such graceful and effortless movements, negate the forceful attack of their opponents. I honestly believed it was all just a well-choreographed performance with no foundation of skill or training. This belief persisted until I attended an Aikido seminar, and the sensei asked me to help demonstrate.

At the time, I had studied karate for eight years. I was in my late teens, in good shape, full of energy, and confident in my abilities. With this misplaced confidence, I willingly accepted the invitation. The sensei told me what techniques he wanted me to perform; I was to attack him with a series of prearranged strikes, which he would, in turn, attempt to avoid.

At first, we moved slowly, but within minutes, our pace increased until we both moved at full speed. I was impressed by the effortless way he managed to negate my attacks. However, I knew the sensei had advance knowledge of my techniques, and I was reluctant to award him too much credit. (As an aside, despite what many might believe, the ability to control another person, even when you know what they are about to do, takes a tremendous amount of skill.)

Always the skeptic, I asked the sensei if it was truly most effective to train by using prearranged techniques. I explained that in karate, we practiced free-form sparring, whereby nothing was prearranged, and both participants were free to use any technique at any time. In other words, it was much more reflective of real-life combat.

He explained that in advanced training, which was not the goal of this seminar, free-form engagement was indeed practiced. He then invited me to spar with him using whatever techniques I desired. I graciously accepted, and we began to spar.

I discovered that the sensei was still able to redirect and negate many of my attacks because his efficient movements enabled him to use my own force against me. I was impressed and a bit embarrassed, but mostly, I was intrigued. I wanted to know how he was able to do what he did and how I, too, could acquire this skill.

He explained that blocking is inefficient because when you move your arm or leg to block a technique, you create an opening that allows your opponent to counterattack. He then explained the concept of Tai Sabaki, a Japanese martial art term referring to whole-body movement or repositioning. It can more easily be understood as efficient body-management, and it is an integral part of the arts of Aikido and Kendo (the art of the sword).

Indeed, all martial arts incorporate some degree of Tai Sabaki because it is a fundamentally sound and efficient way to move. Essentially, Tai Sabaki allows you to avoid an attack by repositioning your body so you can more easily evade and redirect your opponent's strikes instead of meeting them head-on. Tai Sabaki requires excellent timing, efficiency of movement, commitment to the technique, and a great deal of courage - because if you fail to perform the move correctly, the attack will succeed.

Another challenge is that it goes against our natural, reflexive instinct to block.

So how can we benefit from Tai Sabaki? We have already established that the martial arts are a microcosm of the real world. Therefore, the principles found within the arts will always provide us a direct and relevant benefit. For example, I used to confront aggression, physical or verbal, with an equally aggressive response. In effect, I was blocking, hoping that my skills were sufficient to the task. I met force with force and hoped for the best. Remember, hope is not a prudent strategy, which calls to mind another expression "When two tigers fight, one will die, but the other will be crippled." To me, that does not sound very appealing. I have since learned that it is much better to avoid or deflect an attack than to meet it head-on.

I remember the first time I used this approach in a professional setting. I was accosted by my manager regarding a mistake I made while trading stocks. My first thought was to block and counterattack. I considered defending my actions and wanted to highlight the errors of my manager. Although this response was tempting, as controlling my emotions is a daily challenge, I withheld my righteous anger. Instead, I told him I understood why he was upset, said that if I were in his shoes, I'd likely be upset also, and lastly, I explained that he could rely on me to rectify the situation.

Responding in this manner, most assuredly served to redirect the attack. Stating that I understood his position took a great deal of the emotion out of his attack. Additionally, saying that I too would be upset, if I were he, established a personal link between us that further changed the tone of the encounter. Finally, by stating that he could count on me to resolve the issue, I effectively refocused the situation on a resolution, not causation, and blame assignment.

Accepting responsibility, establishing a personal connection, and redirecting focus are verbal forms of Tai Sabaki that you can employ in any type of confrontation. I am sure that we can all recall situations that we handled by blocking and countering. Imagine using this new perspective to reach a more advantageous resolution. Something as simple replying to an attack with words like, "I understand," can advantageously redirect the confrontation.

Takeaway: Do not meet confrontation head-on because, in a battle of strength, you may not have the advantage. Instead, establish a connection and redirect the attack by making the issue solution-oriented; doing so will assuredly take the emotion out of the encounter.

Is That So?

"One does not discover new lands without consenting to lose sight of the shore for a very long time." – *Andre Gide*

Most would likely agree that "A picture is worth a thousand words." While pictures are unquestionably powerful, I believe in the power of words. I believe that the right words strung together properly can convey more clarity and meaning than any picture.

For this reason, I appreciate that many martial art teachings are communicated through the use of allegorical stories, samurai maxims, and Zen koans (paradoxical anecdotes or riddles used in Zen Buddhism to demonstrate the inadequacy of logical reasoning and to provoke enlightenment).

As you read the following passages, keep in mind the expression that "Becoming is better than being," for it speaks to a mindset of continual growth and optimism. Remember also that God always gives us a second chance. It is called tomorrow! Therefore, I encourage you to maintain a positive perspective in all endeavors because it serves as the cornerstone of true happiness and continual progress. Lastly, remember that knowing others is wisdom, knowing oneself is enlightenment. I hope the messages contained herein will provide the enlightenment you seek.

Letting Go

A senior monk and a junior monk were traveling together. At one point, they came to a river with a strong current. As the monks prepared to cross the river, they saw a young and beautiful woman also attempting to cross. The young woman asked if they could help her cross to the other side.

The two monks glanced at one another because they had taken vows not to touch a woman.

Then, without a word, the older monk picked up the woman, carried her across the river, placed her gently on the other side, and carried on his journey.

The younger monk couldn't believe what had just happened. After rejoining his companion, he was speechless, and an hour passed without a word between them.

Two more hours passed, then three, finally, the younger monk could not contain himself any longer and blurted out, "As monks, we are not permitted to touch a woman, how could you carry that woman on your shoulders?"

The older monk looked at him and replied, "Brother, I set her down on the other side of the river. Why are you still carrying her?"

Takeaway: Martial art training teaches us to live in the present, to start fresh and not let the past or the future cloud our minds. When we live in the past or project into the future, we diminish the present, which is where our growth and happiness reside. Let go of all that is not in the now. Remember the adage, "Yesterday is history, tomorrow is a mystery, but today is a gift, that is why we call it the present."

Contempt Prior to Investigation

A beautiful girl in the village was pregnant. Her angry parents demanded to know who fathered the child. At first resistant to confess, the anxious and embarrassed girl finally pointed to Hakuin, the Zen master whom everyone previously revered for living such a pure life. When the outraged parents confronted Hakuin with their daughter's accusation, he simply replied, "Is that so?"

When the child was born, the parents brought it to the Hakuin, who now was viewed as a pariah by the whole village.

They demanded that he take care of the child since it was his responsibility.

"Is that so?" Hakuin said calmly as he accepted the child.

For many months he took very good care of the child until the daughter could no longer withstand the lie she had told. She confessed that the real father was a young man in the village whom she had tried to protect. The parents immediately went to Hakuin to see if he would return the baby. With profuse apologies, they explained what had happened.

"Is that so?" Hakuin said as he handed them the child.

Takeaway: Martial artists do not rely on past performance to predict future results, nor do they revel in praise or wallow in self-pity when facing condemnation. Instead, they face each new encounter with equanimity to ensure that their emotions do not lead to impulsive and improper action.

Therefore, when faced with praise, criticism, or accusation, try to remember Hakuin, and before you react, think to yourself...Is that so? I can assure you that you will find this helpful, perhaps even amusing, but certainly worth the effort.

Chapter XV

Feeling is Believing

"We don't see things as they are, we see them as we are."
– Anais Nin

In addiction groups, the term *a geographical* is sometimes used when a person who wishes to change his or her behavior moves to a new location without addressing the underlying cause. Unfortunately, a move on its own rarely elicits the desired change because, as the expression goes, "Wherever you go, there you are."

Think back to the chapter, "Constant in the Equation." The lesson in that chapter applies here as well because wherever we go, for better or worse, we bring ourselves. Therefore, continually strive to bring your best self as the martial arts masters have so strenuously emphasized. But, bringing your best self and becoming the constant in the equation presupposes that we see things from the proper perspective. And, if you subscribe to the premise in Anais Nin's quote, then you realize that we are faced with yet another paradox.

The paradox is that to succeed in achieving our goals, we need to see situations as they are. However, because our perceptions filter everything we see, how can we hope to view the situation objectively? The answer lies in our ability to intuit the situation by trusting our instincts, rather than our perceptions. The former is internal, the latter external. Seeing is not believing because it is filtered by our past experiences and societal influences. Feeling, however, emerges from the unconscious, innate and ever-present understanding of a situation, in other words, our instinct.

It is well known that horses are extremely sensitive to human emotions. One Swedish study confirmed that horses not only sense the anxiety of their riders but also experience an increased heart rate at the same time as their human companions. This may be why it is said that horses can sense fear when a new human is attempting to handle them.

Additionally, horses can sense where there is a disconnect between what they are seeing and what they are feeling. Said another way, when a person's insides match their outsides, horses become calmer and more trusting. This ability to sense emotions spring from a horse's natural self-defense mechanism. It is their equivalent of intuition because, as prey, horses must rely on instinct to survive.

We, too, are animals, and instincts helped our ancestors survive long before logic and intellect became the lens through which decisions were made. Unfortunately, while logic and intellect are essential tools, they are not the only factors contributing to living a fulfilling life.

When facing an unknown and stressful situation where we do not have the luxury of reasoned analysis, we have only our instinct to guide us. This, however, is not a detriment. Instead, for many of us, it is a long-abandoned gift, displaced in favor of intellect. Ignoring our instinct detrimentally removes one of our most valuable tools out of the toolbox.

The early masters realized this and therefore trained their mind and body to the point where instinct and intellect were coequal parts of their being, not separate, competing components. If we are to become the constant in the equation, and if we are to see things as they are rather than how we perceive them, then we must revert to the point where instinct and intellect are coequals.

The best way to accomplish this is through meditation. Through meditation, we get in touch with our inner, intuitive self. This is not a book on meditative practices; however, I recommend searching for quality books and seminars on the subject. As you learn to meditate and deepen your practice, you will become more in touch with your intuitive nature and more closely unite body and mind.

That said, I would be remiss if I did not offer some personal insight regarding my experience with meditation. The following observations are reflective of my experiences with the meditative process.

- There is no preordained way to meditate; many options and iterations are available.
- Meditation can be practiced under any circumstances; meditation is person-specific much as it is in prayer.
- The very act of attempting to meditate will yield significant benefits.
- Meditation takes us out of our brains, which is the key to intuitive action.
- Mediation is a means through which we can open ourselves to feeling or intuiting situations.
- There is no downside to meditation.

The most common meditation practice is to lie or sit in a comfortable position, close the eyes, and breathe deeply. The prescribed breathing method is to inhale deeply through the nose with the tongue placed on the roof of the mouth, to hold that breath for several seconds, and to release the breath by pushing it out through the mouth with the tongue now placed on the floor of the mouth.

Expect great results, and they will manifest.

Takeaway: Many of us neglect our intuitive, instinctual side and replace it with an emphasis on all things intellectual. This is a serious and potentially dangerous mistake, for it limits our ability to act effectively. If we want to achieve our goals, or simply gain the confidence and peace-of-mind we seek, we must use all our God-given tools. If horses can do it, so can we.

Chapter XVI

Ceding is Conceding

"What's the world's greatest lie? It's this: that at a certain point in our lives, we lose control of what's happening to us, and our lives become controlled by fate." – Paulo Coehlo

Metaphorically, an individual who takes the road less traveled is a person who acts independently, free from the conformity and groupthink that binds the majority. This premise begs the question, why would anyone take the road less traveled, or for that matter, is it beneficial to do so?

It would be disingenuous to state that I know the answer to these questions. However, I can say that over forty years, I have seen many traditional martial artists take the path less traveled by consciously choosing a life of self-discipline, self-denial, and individual responsibility. What drives these choices is a desire for the attainment of self-mastery, a mastery not merely of the physical aspects of the art, but the entire individual: mind, body, and spirit.

The pursuit of self-mastery requires accepting the premise that we, as individuals, have considerable control over our lives. We are not kites blowing in the wind, but the sail that moves the boat. It is our directed effort that makes our goals achievable. While we cannot guarantee the outcome, we can surely influence the result by controlling the inputs. Success may incorporate an element of fate; however, it is our responsibility to consciously make informed decisions to facilitate the desired result.

Our efforts for self-mastery will not bear fruit if we cede responsibility to fate alone. We must continue to make well-reasoned choices and not become apathetic by believing that we are incapable of affecting our destiny. We must instead move toward our goals by consciously and continually managing our effort, dedication, and perseverance.

Recognizing that we control many, but not all, aspects of our lives does not mean abandoning social responsibility. Adherence to societal rules — government regulations, educational standards, etc. — is essential to ensuring a well-functioning society and does not equate to abdicating control over our lives. Failing to appreciate this distinction, however, can create a mindset whereby we cede what we should control, and we attempt to control that which we should accept.

I believe we must make intentional choices in the areas of life where we do have control. Giving up that choice i.e. ceding control is an unwilling or unknowing relinquishment of personal power that must be recognized and avoided; it is the root cause of many of our problems and a surrendering of our power and independence. In other words, it is conceding defeat.

Takeaway: True martial artists take the road less traveled. They consciously choose not to cede control of their immediate lives to outside factors or fate. They can differentiate between conformity, as needed, and ceding control over personal development. They understand that when a person cedes control, they concede defeat. Therefore, let us follow the martial way and not live the world's greatest lie. Let us choose the road less traveled.

Chapter XVII

Wisdom to Go

"It's not who you are that holds you back; it's who you think you are not." – Denis Waitley

This chapter contains several quotes that I love because they are Zen-like yet easily understood and relevant to our journey. Zen is an integral part of the martial arts; it provides the discipline and singleness of thought and action that martial artists need to overcome adversity. To this point, we should remain mindful that all life inherently involves conflict; the only thing that changes is the battlefield. Thus, we must remain vigilant in the way we view situations and interpersonal encounters lest we fall prey to the unproductive, negative thinking that keeps us from reaching our potential!

LESSONS FROM THE DOJO

Here then, are four quotes that may help you acquire the mindset needed to overcome detrimental emotions and provide you with the necessary insight to improve your interpersonal interactions.

1. "Shortcuts generally get you nowhere faster." - Sensei Hitoshi

All I can add to this salient quote is the familiar truism that the only place where Success comes before Work is in the dictionary,

2. "You can appreciably improve your skills by acquiring ten years of progressive experience, or you can stagnate by acquiring one year of experience which you repeat for the next nine years." – Sensei Pete

People often share with me how many years of martial arts training they have, or for how long they have worked in a particular capacity. In theory, this should equate to a continually increasing skill level and a corresponding increase in knowledge; ideally, each day, month, or year spent performing an action will result in appreciably improved performance.

This, however, is often not the case. Instead, whether through laziness, ignorance, or lack of mentoring, we do not see a progressive increase in ability but instead witness stagnation, or worse yet, skill degradation. To grow in knowledge and ability, our learning must be progressive. We cannot merely repeat actions and expect marked improvement. Instead, we must repeatedly renew our commitment to holistically improving ourselves in mind, body, and spirit. We must strive to create a mindset that enables us to conquer negative emotions like fear and self-doubt and helps us make more informed decisions where we respond rather than react to situations.

In other words, maintain a healthy degree of cynicism when hearing about another's extensive experience; we must be mindful not to fall into the same trap ourselves. Time, and productive time, are two entirely different things. We gain the most benefit when we seek to continually renew our commitment to improving ourselves rather than being lulled by and embracing the familiar.

3. "Share don't show." – Ed Parker

Good teachers can show you how to do things. Great teachers can share with you the how and the why behind the things you do. When teaching others, aspire to follow the model of sharing, not showing, because, by sharing, you enhance the experience for all parties. This concept is eloquently stated in a quote by Sensei Ed Parker, one of the early American martial art pioneers. Sensei Parker said, "I am not going to show you my art. I am going to share it with you. If I show it to you it becomes an exhibition, and in time it will be pushed so far into the back of your mind that it will be lost. But by sharing it with you, you will not only retain it forever, but I too will improve."

I believe that if you can only show, but not explain a technique, then you really do not know it. If I were to be generous in this regard, I might grant that a person may know whatever it is they are trying to teach, but that they truly do not understand it. Understanding is the key to sharing knowledge with others.

Therefore, I only teach what I truly understand and can explain. This concept applies not just to martial arts, but to anything we try to teach. Moreover, we, as teachers, do not need to personally be able to perform the technique, draw the picture, or play the instrument, to be able to understand and teach it.

For example, boxing trainer Angelo Dundee successfully trained Muhammad Ali, whom many consider the greatest heavyweight boxer of all time, not because he was able to get in the ring and spar with Muhammad, but because he understood and could share with him his extensive boxing knowledge.

4. "Respond, don't react." – Unknown
Martial artists train their minds and bodies to respond to stimuli in very efficient and measured ways. Through continuous repetition of properly performed, physically

sound techniques, a martial artist's actions become more of a response than a reaction, which begs the question, what is the difference?

The difference is that a reaction is an unplanned, random act performed without conscious thought, much like a blink reflex. Reactions are not fundamentally bad. In truth, they are part of the body's natural self-defense mechanism. That said, they are uninformed actions, lacking the benefit of reasoned efficiency. For example, if I were to throw a punch at an untrained person, their reaction will most likely be random, inefficient, and suboptimal. The stimuli, my punch, caused a likely ineffective reaction from them because there was nothing innately informed driving their movement.

In contrast, let's say I throw a punch at an experienced martial artist or boxer. Using the same stimuli, I would witness a quicker, more efficient, and more effective result. They would counter my punch with an informed response. Training the mind and body to deal with diverse inputs properly results in a more effective output.

The concept of responding vs. reacting applies to every facet of our lives. For example, if our boss, spouse, parent, etc. were to yell at us, and we immediately grew angry and yelled back, did we respond or react? We reacted. A response is an informed action to an external stimulus, not a knee-jerk reaction.

Therefore, if we want to interact more productively in our personal or professional endeavors, we must create a pause between the input and the output. The pause will provide the opportunity for an informed response, but we must discipline ourselves to achieve this result. Encouragingly, just being aware of the difference is a great start, and each time we succeed in this practice, we move closer to reducing the negative consequences of impulsive reactions.

About the Author

Peter Tocco, a.k.a. Sensei Pete, has trained in the martial arts for more than 40 years, utilizing its physical, mental, and philosophical principles to enhance his life and those of his students.

The discipline derivative of his training enabled him to advance his professional career across a broad spectrum of high profile positions, including as a special agent with the United States Justice and the U.S. Treasury Departments, as a management consultant, and as a Wall Street financial services professional; he received his MBA from the *Wharton School of Business*.

To preview upcoming books please visit
www.petertoccoauthor.com

To access Sensei Pete's blog please visit
www.thekaratesensei.com

Personal Note

In early 2020 I founded *Martial Art Miracles Inc.,* a not-for-profit organization that teaches martial art skills to children with developmental disabilities.

I believe that just like with the wisdom contained within the martial arts, the physical skills and mental discipline that can be acquired through training is beneficial to any practitioner regardless of ability or disability.

Therefore, if you are interested in learning more about *Martial Art Miracles*, or if you know someone that may benefit from its services, or if you are interested in donating your time or resources to furthering its mission, please visit us at

www.martialartmiracles.org

Additional Gift

As a lifelong martial artist and former federal law enforcement officer, I take great care to ensure that those closest to me are well-informed and capable of handling themselves in difficult situations.

To this end, I have created **Situational Awareness** courses that will help you, your family, and anyone for whom you are responsible stay safe and live free from fear. Situational Awareness training will help you become more aware of the things that you do, or fail to do, that increase your chances of becoming a victim.

The courses are designed as <u>PowerPoint-driven lectures</u> to make it convenient and accessible to any audience. You can choose to have a live, in-person presentation, a virtual Zoom presentation, (both of which are interactive), or you can simply purchase and download the desired course using the link below.

To ensure that as many as possible benefit from this training, I am offering my readers a **15% discount** on all *Situational Awareness Courses.* Upon purchase you will be sent a discount code which you can apply to the desired course.

To purchase your Situational Awareness course or to find additional information regarding Situational Awareness training, please visit

<u>www.capitalenterprisesconsulting.com</u>.

www.ingramcontent.com/pod-product-compliance
Lightning Source LLC
LaVergne TN
LVHW041231080426

835508LV00011B/1153